ON THE SHOULDERS OF GIANTS

Contents

Also includes
On the shoulders of Giants DVD

ISBN: 978-1-910335-02-4

First published in 2014 by Trinity Mirror

and

Liverpool City Council
Municipal Buildings
Dale Street
Liverpool L2 2DH

British Library cataloguing-in-publication information
A British Library CIP record is available for this title

Printed and bound in the UK by Buxton Press

Mayor of Liverpool welcome

In April 2012, three Giant visitors captured our hearts, our minds and our imaginations.

The reaction to their first three-day Liverpool adventure was overwhelming – we always knew it would be a visual spectacular, but the way in which hundreds of thousands of people emotionally connected with these towering figures was unexpectedly moving.

Their impact was not only felt across the city, but it resonated across the region, and was picked up around the world.

No sooner had those much-loved Giants sailed away down the Mersey, we received a barrage of emails, letters and phone calls asking when they would return.

The simple story of a young girl searching for her father struck a chord with everyone regardless of their age or gender. We urged her forward on her journey, marvelling at her joy in walking the streets of Liverpool, laughing at the antics of mischievous Xolo and applauding, in some cases weeping, when she was reunited with her uncle.

There was no question. They had to return.

One of the main reasons why Sea Odyssey was such an unprecedented success in 2012 was the story. A hugely emotive part of our own history, it was essential we commemorated the 100 years since the sinking of the Titanic in a sensitive, and at the same time, memorable and creative way. Without a doubt, Sea Odyssey achieved this.

We had to ensure when the Giants returned, that once again it wouldn't just be about three unusual characters roaming our city – they had to be here to tell a story people could relate to.

Liverpool's reaction to the outbreak of World War One was the right tale to tell – especially as it linked in to the national and global story.

The role of the Liverpool Pals had, sadly, become forgotten by many over the years. We knew that by working with Jean-Luc and all our friends at Royal de Luxe again, we could shine a spotlight on this remarkable piece of our city's history.

It could be a story from the silver screen: war breaks out and a call is made for volunteers. Friends, neighbours and colleagues are asked to sign up, standing side by side as they fight for their country. Within days, 1,500 men enlist with more signing up in the months that followed. Excited by the adventure that lay ahead of them, many believed they would be home by Christmas. But sadly, thousands were never to return.

In July this tragic tale, which engendered a sense of pride in our city, came alive. Flashmobs called out for volunteers and the resulting battalion marched with pride along our waterfront, in costume and character.

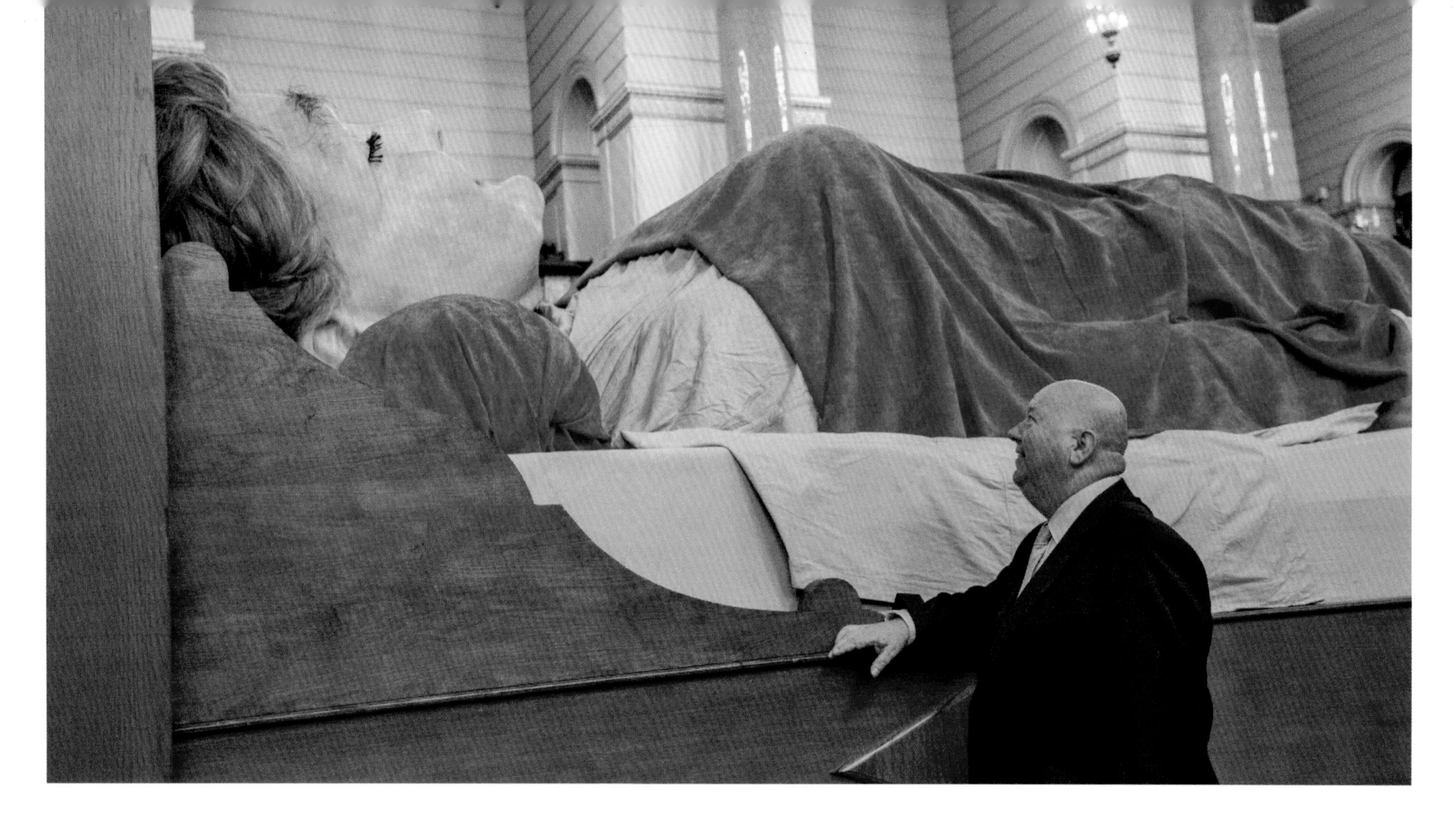

Actors recreated the scenes, and interspersed with these were the real-life memories of elderly people from Liverpool who recalled how World War One affected their families and communities.

When one of these stories played out on Saturday morning in Newsham Park a hush fell across the many thousands gathered. Hearing an old man break down as he recollected how his Grandmother was told of her son's death in battle, only to receive a letter from him days later which he had sent before he had been killed, was heart-breaking.

Stories like these should never be forgotten. We should never forget the sacrifices made for us a century ago, and which have continued to be made to the present day.

Our three Giant friends helped make this happen. A new audience, old and young, was reached, and it was even bigger than 2012.

We were entertained. We were moved. We were awe-struck once more.

And with the help of this beautiful book and DVD, you can re-live those special memories time and time again.

Joe Anderson OBE
Mayor of Liverpool

T.W.LEW
STATIONERY PRINTI

The Giants return with a poignant message

As part of a co-commission between Liverpool City Council and 14-18 NOW, the official cultural programme for the First World War centenary commemorations, Jean-Luc Courcoult's amazing production told the story of the Liverpool Pals Regiment and reproduced genuine Liverpudlian memories about the march to war in 1914.

When war broke out on 4 August, it was greeted with scenes of wild enthusiasm on both banks of the Mersey and across the land. Young men from all social backgrounds rushed to join the army. Recruitment offices opened in nearly every town and city.

The mood was one of patriotism – perhaps spurred by a notion, which seemed to have spread from nowhere, that an easy victory would be secured by Christmas.

On 8 August, one local newspaper echoed this sentiment under the headlines 'The War: Local Patriotism Aflame' and 'Birkonians Abroad: Exciting Experiences'.

Men and boys, rich and poor stepped up to the challenge, and nowhere was that mood stronger than in Liverpool, then regarded as the second port of the mighty British Empire.

Many of the young men wished to serve in the army alongside their friends and colleagues from work. This led to the formation of the Liverpool Pals – with similar battalions, such as the Grimsby Chums, quickly following in at least 50 towns.

Behind the idea was hard realism. Lord Herbert Kitchener, Secretary of State for War, had not been carried away by the euphoria. He knew Germany was a terrible foe with a huge army and he feared the fighting would be long and brutal.

He needed as many men to sign up as possible – and was convinced the 710,000 in the British Army at the start of 1914 would not be enough.

The rallying cry for volunteers went out – the slogan on the famous poster of the Field Marshal pointing read: 'Britons: Lord Kitchener Wants You. Join Your Country's Army! God Save The King'.

General Sir Henry Rawlinson suggested to Kitchener that the recruitment drive would be aided if men from the same offices could enlist together. This idea was adopted by Lord Derby who had an estate in Knowsley.

Lord Derby said: "This should be a battalion of pals, a battalion in which friends from the same office fight shoulder to shoulder for the honour of Britain and the credit of Liverpool."

He also wrote to employers asking that they encourage their employees to enlist. Volunteers were asked to turn up at the headquarters of the King's Liverpool Regiment on St Anne Street at 7.30pm on 28 August.

The sheer number of men who turned up overwhelmed the recruiting hall and extra rooms had to be opened to deal with all the men who wanted to enlist. A battalion usually consisted of between 800 and 1,000 men. Within two days 1,500 men volunteered.

The 17th Battalion was formed, and within days three more service battalions – the 18th, 19th and 20th, all attached to the King's Regiment – were established.

In total more than 5,000 men volunteered to be Liverpool Pals. These men took part in some of the bloodiest battles of the war.

The Pals saw their first action at the Battle of the Somme and lost 300 men on that fateful first day.

From then on they fought all through the Somme and went on to The Battle of Arras and the muddy hell of Passchendaele in 1917. More than 2,800 were never to return home and many more were wounded.

The Liverpool Pals will always be remembered as friends, colleagues and relations who joined up together, served together and, sadly for so many of them, died together.

A permanent memorial to their sacrifice now stands proudly inside Lime Street Station.

A Liverpool love story

It all began again with a phone call…

When we said goodbye to this amazing piece of street theatre in 2012 there was a sense that there was somehow some unfinished business. There was a swell of emotion from the people of Liverpool for not just days and weeks, but months after the event which only added to the notion that there was more to come.

But it had to be right. The timing and the story.

Royal de Luxe's reputation for the creation of stunning performances was at an all-time high, partly thanks to their work in Liverpool in 2012. Countries from across the world were knocking on the door of our French friends, eager for them to bring their magic to their particular city.

The UK was no different – decision makers had seen the impact the show had on Liverpool and they wanted to experience the 'Giant' effect. Luckily for us, Liverpool held a very special place in Jean-Luc's heart. He wanted to come back. And he picked up the phone and made the call.

A new Giant with 100 years of history in her eyes was bound for Liverpool and a new giant chapter began. She was beautiful.

I was lucky enough to see her being created – it took one person a whole year to make her beautifully crafted hands, the colour of her skin resulted in much debate and I won't even get into the endless conversations about her slippers and their sheepskin lining...

The detail and finesse that went into this process was simply awe-inspiring. This wasn't just a marionette to parade around a city. Her creators were making another member of their family, and to witness the love and dedication that went into this latest addition was humbling. It was true artistry at work.

Over the months following that phone call, the story evolved. Tony Hollingsworth from the Liverpool Pals Memorial Fund, Lord Derby and countless others came together to create the backstory for our next Giant journey.

Jean-Luc visited care homes across the city meeting elderly members of our community who with their own words entranced him with their memories of memories. These recordings were transformed into beautiful soliloquies, bringing the city's war stories to life throughout the event.

It was an emotional five days. The work that goes into an event of this scale is immense and admittedly, there was a brief moment during the event when I asked myself the question – why do we do it?

But within minutes my question was answered. In Newsham Park I looked round at the tens of thousands of people gathered – people from all walks of life who had come out with their families and friends, and not only let their imaginations run wild but let a bit of much-needed magic into their lives. It really was a privilege to be part of a team that made this happen.

This show was about memories, and here we were, creating new memories which people would re-tell for years to come.

The world was looking at Liverpool and we showed the city at its very best, a city that finds new ways to share its history whilst creating memories for future generations.

So what next for Liverpool?

In 2015 it's all about the river and our connection to the waterfront and the world. What is now a £32 billion cruise passenger industry started from this city with the humble beginnings of a Royal Mail ship and a live cow on board to provide milk for the passengers.

Two major events to mark the 175th anniversary of Cunard will bring the Pier Head to life in glorious technicolor. In May, three Cunard queens pay homage to the city that gave them life and in July we welcome renowned fashion designer Wayne Hemmingway as Creative Director for a vintage inspired recreation of the first transatlantic crossing.

At the heart of these is the International Mersey River Festival, brought back into the city's events calendar by the Mayor in 2011, and which has grown every year.

This city will always respond to creativity and great artists are in its DNA. The story of Liverpool will always be reinvigorated by its major events and its cultural infrastructure.

These help tell the city's story to the world - and with Liverpool's immense history we are only at the beginning. It's exciting to think what the next chapter will bring.

Claire McColgan MBE
Director, Culture Liverpool

Royal de Luxe: Merci et à bientôt

Royal de Luxe's first Liverpool experience was an unforgettable one for the entire company.

Despite their 35 years in the street theatre world and their immense global popularity, it was rare for them to receive such a reaction from an audience similar to the one they enjoyed in April 2012.

From the moment crowds began to gather around the slumbering Little Girl Giant and her dog, Xolo, in Stanley Park, the anticipation was tangible. The people of Liverpool, and the thousands who travelled from outside the city's boundaries, were ready to embrace what the three days ahead held in store.

Sea Odyssey saw the Little Girl Giant, Xolo and the Uncle Diver Giant became part of Liverpool's diverse and vibrant creative history.

These French artists had brought magic to the city's streets and the results left a lasting impression on both sides of the English Channel.

In 2013, Founder and Artistic Director, Jean-Luc Courcoult, began to let his imagination run wild again.

It was time for a new addition to the Giant family.

Looking at all the options, he soon hit upon the idea of a Grandmother Giant and there was no going back. It's always a risk to introduce something new to an already successful formula, but fans were familiar with the existing Giants and he wanted that element of surprise for audiences.

MEPHISTO
JOAILLIER
HORLOGER
A&D
A&D

For months on end, a team of up to 70 people worked on creating the new character, using different materials and techniques. And slowly but surely, the Grandmother Giant began to come to life.

When completed, the 85 year old would stand at nearly eight metres tall, and when she couldn't stand (she is a pensioner after all), a five tonne wheelchair would help her on her journey.

Not only was this going to be a new addition to the family, but there was going to be something different about this Giant.

She would be able to talk - although not in any language we would understand. Through an interpreter she would tell tales about the world, passing on her knowledge to the hundreds of thousands of eager listeners.

Jean-Luc's vision was for the Grandmother Giant to have a definitive personality. She'd be tough, daring and mischievous.

Not caring for social graces, she would happily slug from her hip-flask of whisky, smoke her pipe and even break wind in public.

But despite her dubious habits, her creator knew people would immediately take the Grandmother Giant to their hearts and hoped people would see something of their own family in this new creation.

While the team busily worked on the new addition, Jean-Luc re-ignited his relationship with Liverpool.

The centenary of the outbreak of World War One was on the horizon and he knew it was the perfect place where a fitting tribute could be made.

Following meetings with the Mayor of Liverpool, Joe Anderson, and Culture Liverpool Director, Claire McColgan, Jean-Luc's focus honed in on the extraordinary story of the Liverpool Pals.

He knew immediately this was the story to tell. And he also knew of an octogenarian lady who would be the perfect storyteller. The latest creation was to get her first outing in Royal de Luxe's hometown Nantes in June, just a month before her star turn in Liverpool.

The show in Nantes called The Planck Wall was a triumph. The French audience embraced the new Giant and her stories of Nantes, its history and connection with the slave trade.

Her inaugural performance hailed a success – she was ready for Liverpool. And Liverpool was more than ready for her.

From the moment she was discovered asleep in St George's Hall, people were hooked. For the five days that followed, Royal de Luxe's hopes were fulfilled. Audiences connected with the Grandmother Giant – they listened to her tales and laughed at her cheeky antics.

The combination of her and the already familiar Little Girl Giant and Xolo was street theatre gold.

Each day, the crowds grew in size, as did Jean-Luc's legendary status – autograph and 'selfie' requests with the man behind this magnificent piece of theatre were in high demand.

When the Giants departed, it was a chance for the French team to reflect on their latest accomplishment.

Once again they had felt an amazing connection with the Liverpool audience. The cheers of delight, the spontaneous applause and the moments of respectful silence had meant all the hard work had been worth it.

They had walked miles around the city which had begun to feel like a second home, and they were going to miss it.

From Liverpool, the Grandmother Giant went to Limerick, and from Limerick... well who knows.

With global interest in Royal de Luxe and their reputation for staging staggering Giant shows, there is a long, long list of cities across the world which want a sprinkle of that Giant magic on their doorstep.

Liverpool has been lucky enough to experience that magic twice. And those events will live long in the memories and hearts of those who saw three Giant visitors beautifully recreate part of our history in truly spectacular style.

"Why do I feel a deep connection with Liverpool? I could sum it up as a love story." ***Jean-Luc Courcoult***

A Grandmother, Planck wall and the Milky Way

A sleeping Grandmother Giant travels through space between two clouds of the Milky Way.

Her mind sails from a star to another whereas her body already arrived at its place of destination and rests laying down in a bed. She lives behind the big explosion which took place 13.7 billion years ago and which our physicists will call the Big Bang.

In this immense unknown area live the Giants. However just before the crossing she is undertaking, she must cross the "Planck wall"*. She often made this route; alone or accompanied by other Giants who land in different eras of the planet. For all, the journey is short: it only takes two days.

At the very beginning, beyond the wall, lies the kingdom of the hereafter, the one in which the soul of our ancestors float for eternity.

Behind her an immense safe wanders in the cosmos. Inside files full of memories pile up. It is the safe of memories of the Grandmother Giant. The pile of files tells the past, the present and the future of Liverpool.

This Grandmother is a queen. Some say that she may have ancient origins from Nantes or Ireland…

She simply comes, like any grandmother, to tell stories by the fire to the people of the city as it used to be done in our countryside. She knows so many things about life, like the ancients who are today lost in our civilisation, marred by their silence. She comes with one of her children for whom she had a small piece of galaxy built with tools that were at hand, so that the child could wake and fall asleep peacefully…

In Liverpool, she will tell us the story of these happy people who went away in 1914 with the King's Regiment, their hope brimming with courage to save the ideal of their time. And then, she will go away through space again in a big floating coffin, to the "Planck wall".

But she will return…

Jean-Luc Courcoult
© Author, Artistic Director & Founder of Royal de Luxe

** All the current cosmology rests on the general relativity theory conceived by Einstein. He did not support the idea of an expanding universe, he considered it as stable.*

Georges Lemaître is the real originator of the Big Bang theory with the assistance of the equations of Einstein, he is the founder of the modern cosmology. Max Planck, Nobel Prize of physics in 1918, is one of the founders of quantum physics (particle physics).

The story of the Big Bang begins after the era of Planck, the Planck wall being the boundary. Planck wall is therefore the limit of the knowledge of the universe.

Wednesday and Thursday 23 – 24 July 2014

Well, wouldn't you be tired after a long journey travelling through time?

On two baking hot days at the height of summer, 42,000 people headed to St George's Hall for a sneak peek of the Grandmother Giant as she snoozed ahead of her adventure around the streets of Liverpool.

The Liverpool Pals regiment was recruited in the very same building so it was only right and proper that the Grandmother paid her own tribute to those soldiers by starting her journey in this city gem.

Young and old stood in awe as they walked around Liverpool's favourite pensioner while, outside, Lord Kitchener appeared from nowhere and called on passers-by to do their patriotic duty and sign up to fight in World War One.

Had Liverpool been hit by a time-warp?

The city braced itself for a breath-taking weekend.

Il y a 13,7
milliards d'années
c'est le Big Bang !
Il y a 4,5
milliards d'années
apparition du Soleil

EX

SPQL

Friday 25 July 2014

The day had arrived that everyone had been waiting for.

The Grandmother Giant, Xolo and the Little Girl Giant would at long last get to stretch their gigantic legs across Liverpool.

The Little Girl Giant and Xolo started their day with a wake-up call at the Planck wall at the entrance to the Queensway Tunnel before making their way through the city centre.

They wowed huge crowds before arriving at the Chinese Arch. It was hot and hard work for the pair so they stopped for a siesta as thousands took photos and stood, open-mouthed, and admired Royal de Luxe's fantastic artistry.

Meanwhile, the Grandmother Giant, wide awake now after her slumber in St George's Hall, gave an impassioned speech to the crowds and then made her way to the Town Hall.

She might be 85 but she was raring to go as she headed to the waterfront and a visit to Salthouse Dock.

After an afternoon snooze, the Grandmother Giant fancied a walk, heading out of the city through Kensington, before arriving – weary, but happy – at Newsham Park on a sun-kissed evening filled with magic.

After waking up outside the Chinese Arch, the Little Girl Giant and Xolo were refreshed and ready to go again, as they too headed out of the city centre.

They took a ticket to ride through Toxteth and Kensington to the beautiful Newsham Park, where the Little Girl Giant and Xolo finally met the Grandmother Giant.

The day had been wonderfully thrilling. Where would the Giants head tomorrow?

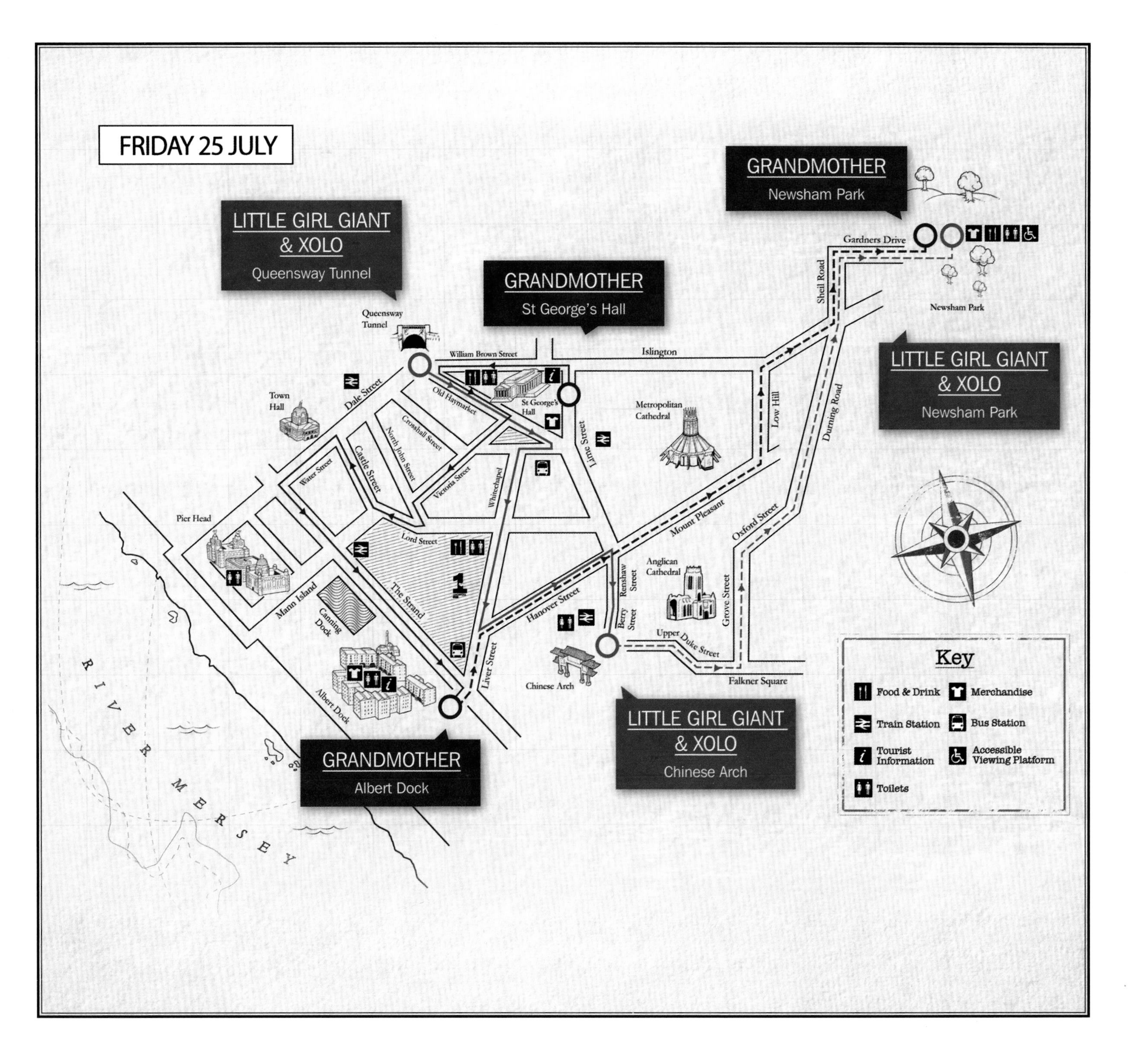

FRIDAY 25 JULY
LITTLE GIRL GIANT & XOLO
Queensway Tunnel
GRANDMOTHER
St George's Hall
GRANDMOTHER
Newsham Park
LITTLE GIRL GIANT & XOLO
Newsham Park
GRANDMOTHER
Albert Dock
LITTLE GIRL GIANT & XOLO
Chinese Arch
Queensway Tunnel
William Brown Street
Islington
Gardners Drive
Newsham Park
Sheil Road
Town Hall
Dale Street
Old Haymarket
St George's Hall
Lime Street
Metropolitan Cathedral
Low Hill
Durning Road
Crosshall Street
North John Street
Castle Street
Water Street
Victoria Street
Whitechapel
Pier Head
Lord Street
Mount Pleasant
Oxford Street
Mann Island
Canning Dock
The Strand
Hanover Street
Renshaw Street
Anglican Cathedral
Grove Street
Berry Street
Upper Duke Street
Falkner Square
Liver Street
Chinese Arch
Albert Dock
RIVER MERSEY
Key
Food & Drink
Merchandise
Train Station
Bus Station
Tourist Information
Accessible Viewing Platform
Toilets

EMPIRE THEATRE
Birkenhead
Wallasey
Southport

"YOUR COUNTRY NEEDS
YOU"

SCHEDULE

27 3400
43
le street
TO LET
SHOP TO LET
ALL ENQUIRIES
BROOK STREET
NERO

ALBERT DOCK
WHISKY
KILBEGGAN

LIVERPOOL
LIVERPOOL
LIVERPOOL

Yale

Yale

ARTIBVS LEGIBVS CONSILIIS
10

BOLD
STREET

whisc
Women's Health Information & Support Centre
20
ZONE
DAPPER
soul cafe
SuttonKersh
To Let
0151 207 9339
take-outs
AUTOMATIC BOLLARDS
ONE Vehicle may proceed
PIERCING

The BLACKIE
Thanks to everyone who buys lottery tickets
The National Lottery
中國城

Cash
Machine Service
THE ARCH

We do not want art for a few
anymore than education for a few
or freedom for a few
ENERGY
COFFEE

camobile
Lebara
OFF LI
Calvin Klein

ARRIVA

HIGHWAY MAINTENANCE

ARRIVA
ARRIVA
ARRIVA
BM-640-JB

THERE IS STILL
A PLACE IN THE LINE
FOR
YOU
THIS
SPACE
IS
RESERVED
FOR
A
FIT
MAN
Will you
fill it?

YOUR COUNTRY NEEDS
YOU

PAISTE

WHISKY
KILBEGGAN

Saturday 26 July 2014

After a busy first day touring the streets of the city, the three Giants slept soundly in Newsham Park.

Another blistering day dawned and Liverpool's favourite trio of tourists walked into the city centre together before the Little Girl Giant and Xolo made their way back to the Planck Wall.

Meanwhile, the Grandmother Giant arrived at the magnificent St George's Hall.

After an afternoon nap, the Little Girl Giant and Xolo, fully refreshed, made their way around the city before meeting at Mann Island and onwards to their next overnight stay at Clarence Dock.

The Giants arrived to huge cheers, and a few tears, as the family rounded the day off with a poignant story and a beautifully cheoreographed dance which mesmerised the thousands gathered.

Finally, the dust settled on another amazing day of drama and emotion.

There was one thing on the lips of everyone in the city – the Giants. And there was still another day of entertainment ahead.

SATURDAY 26 JULY

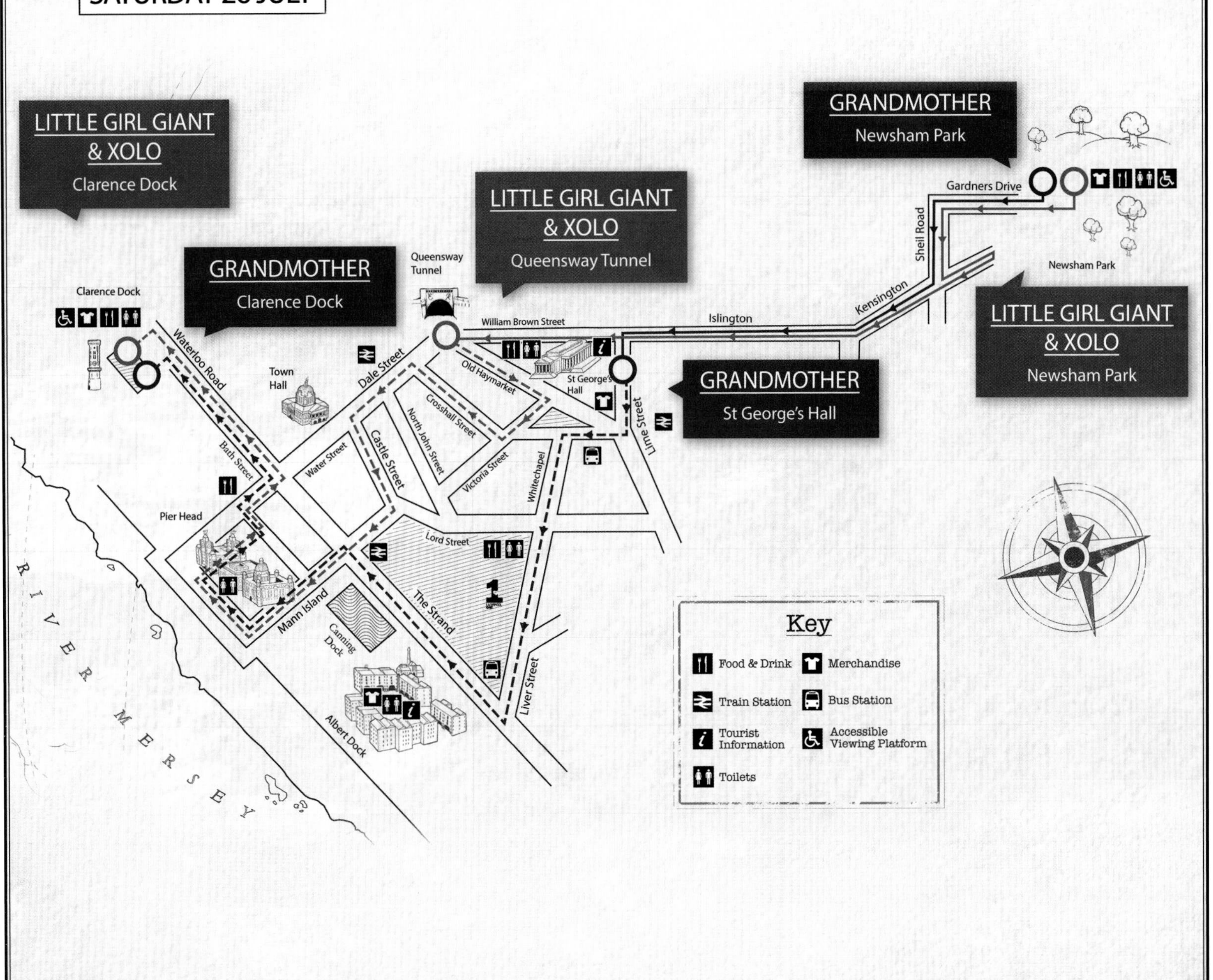

Yale

TEREX

XG274

Free Cash
Machine
Service

HIYA
GIANTS

Raz Newsagents

WINE CROSS
WINE CROSS
OPEN TILL LATE
WINE CROSS
TATTOO

MUSEUM

ALL ENQUIRIES
100,000 SQ FT

SPOON
LUSH SPA
LUSH
WONGS
AMBULANCE
HELP POINT

49903

SHORT
TERM
HIRE

HOLDERS

JCB

Sunday 27 July 2014

After travelling nearly 30 miles during the three days of action (not counting the 14 billion years it took them to reach Liverpool from a time before the start of the Universe), the Giants bid the city farewell with the tears and cheers of thousands of spectators ringing in their ears.

Following a restful night's sleep at Clarence Dock, the three Giants made their final journey along the Strand where they walked together past the Three Graces and towards Albert Dock.

In parade formation, they were joined by a Liverpool Pals battalion who had volunteered to fight for their country. As they marched past the thousands spectating broke out in huge spontaneous applause.

Recreating the 2012 departure, the Giants made their exit from Liverpool on the River Mersey, jumping on board a ship at Canning Dock.

Marching bands, complete with pipers helped entertain the massive crowds and added yet another dimension to an event that had thrilled, shocked and surprised in equal measure.

Bidding farewell to the city who had taken them to its heart, the Giants eventually sailed away over the horizon and off to another land.

Once again Liverpool had embraced this spectacular event and the special visitors would live long in the hearts and minds of everyone lucky enough to be part of their magical journey.

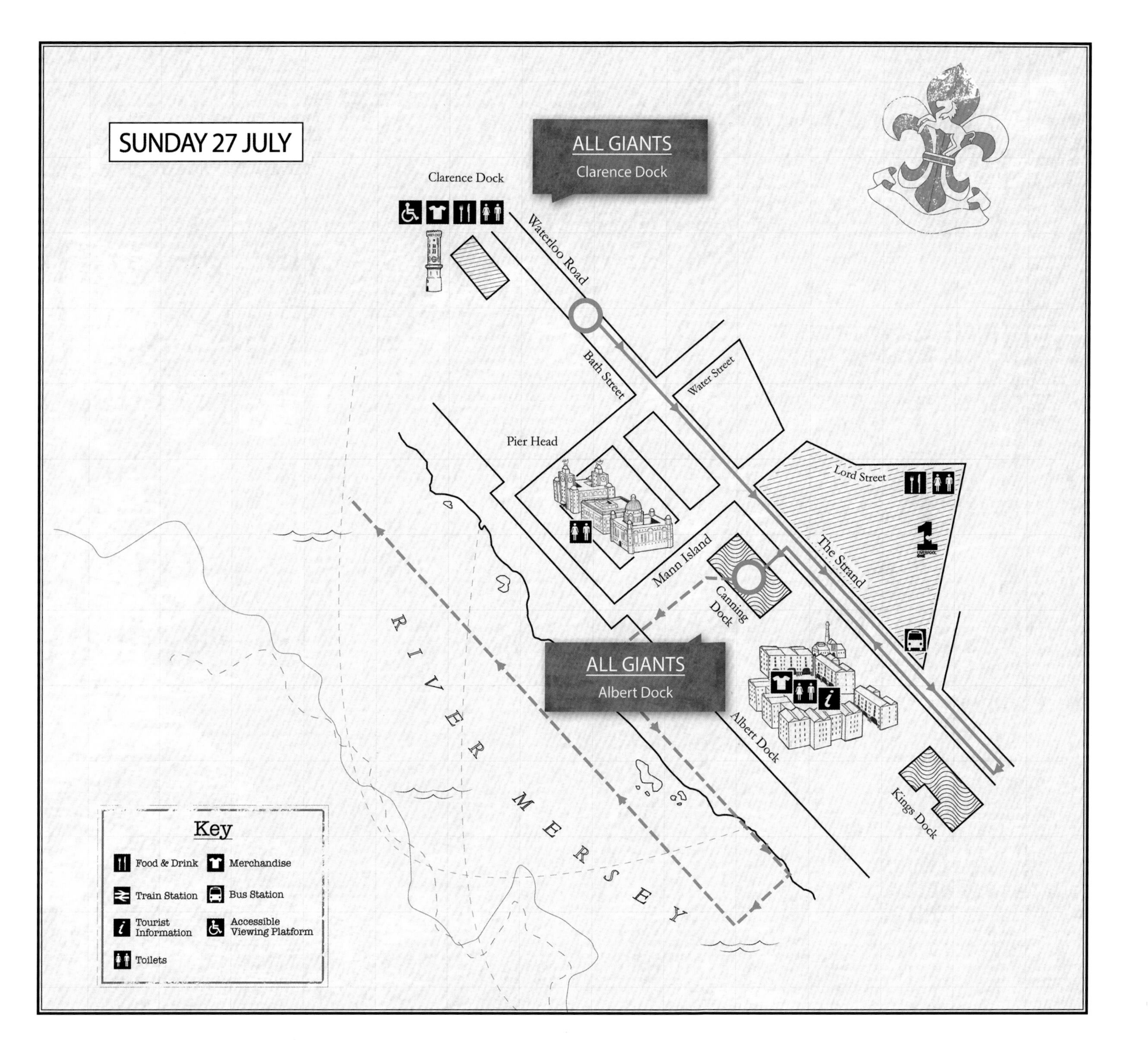

SUNDAY 27 JULY
ALL GIANTS
Clarence Dock
Clarence Dock
Waterloo Road
Bath Street
Water Street
Pier Head
Lord Street
Mann Island
The Strand
Canning Dock
ALL GIANTS
Albert Dock
RIVER MERSEY
Albert Dock
Kings Dock
Key
Food & Drink
Merchandise
Train Station
Bus Station
Tourist Information
Accessible Viewing Platform
Toilets

Pier Head
Terminal
(I.O.M. & Dublin)

PIER HEAD

WELCOME TO

TATE
TATE

-WELCOME TO-
MARITIME

HULL

THE
PUMPHOUSE
MERSEYSIDE MARITIME MUSEUM
HULL

Photographers

On behalf of all who read this book, a heartfelt thank you goes to all the photographers for their stunning images, without which, this book would not exist.

Ant Clausen (commissioned by Liverpool City Council)

New Zealand-born, self-taught photographer Ant Clausen started his professional career 30m under water, filming sharks in Australia and Egypt. Seven years later, he is based in Liverpool, making the most of his love of photography by capturing people, places, events and local colour. From the Queen to Liverpool's International Mersey River Festival and Music on the Waterfront series, Ant's laid-back approach effortlessly captures a look that says it all and infuses each image with a little 'Kiwi-magic'. Recent work in Argentina for Condé Nast has broadened his photographic horizon and inspired him for future work abroad, but for now he is more than content to call Liverpool home. His work can be viewed at ***antclausen.com***

Mark McNulty (commissioned by Liverpool City Council)

Mark McNulty's vast portfolio chronicles the people and culture of Liverpool since the late 1980s and offers a unique insight into the life of the city. His work, exhibited and published widely throughout the UK and on an international platform, is a blend of music, arts, events, advertising and portraiture that documents the city and its people. In 2008 his book 'Pop Cultured' was published by Liverpool University Press, celebrating 20 years of music photography and featuring some of the biggest names in music. His regular Liverpool blog, recognised as a 'must read' by the Guardian, can be found at ***rivercool.co.uk***, and his portfolio and archive can be viewed at ***markmcnulty.co.uk***

Pete Carr (commissioned by Liverpool City Council)

Described as 'the 21st century Chambré Hardman' in a review of his Port of Culture exhibition, Pete Carr is one of the most prominent photographers in Liverpool today. His work has been featured nationally and internationally by clients such as Cunard, the Guardian, National Museums Liverpool, The Boston Globe, Open Eye Gallery, Tate Liverpool and the National Media Museum in Bradford. His love of street photography, portraiture, architecture and documenting events in and around Liverpool is catalogued on his award winning photoblog *littletimemachine.com*, which recently celebrated its 10th birthday and highlights are included in his book 'Port of Culture'. Pete works as a commercial and editorial photographer and can be contacted via his website ***petecarr.net***

Contributing Photographers

Anthony Babonneau, Steph Chester, Ian Cooper, Paul Daniels, Chris Deeney, Maria Fetherstone, Martin Gray, Ian Greenall, Dave Gore, Michael Holden, Danny Jackson, Valéry Joncheray, Gareth Jones, Kevin Kelly, Serge Koutchinsky, Colin Lane, Karen Larmour, Bernie MacDonald, James Maloney, Brian Mason, Steve Marmion, Jenny McNulty, Christopher Middleton, Mike Price, Tim Smith, Andrew Teebay, Victoria Tetley, Gavin Trafford, Andy J Walker, Tracy Wilkinson, Richard Williams, Pascal Victor.

Acknowledgements

Memories of August 1914 was co-comissioned by Liverpool City Council and 14-18 NOW and we would like to thank all the staff across the council who worked tirelessly to bring this show to the streets of Liverpool.

We would also like to thank all the members of Royal de Luxe who travelled to Liverpool, the artistry and commitment they demonstrated was truly spectacular.

Finally, Liverpool City Council would also like to extend a massive thank you to all our partners, volunteers and the people of Liverpool whose support made this event such a tremendous success. The list of those we personally wish to thank is endless. We would like to take this opportunity to thank all those groups and individuals who made our oversized visitors feel at home, with a special nod to those communities around the park who went that extra mile to make sure three French Giants received a warm scouse welcome.

For further information on events in Liverpool, follow Culture Liverpool via

itsliverpool.com/culture

facebook.com/cultureliverpool

@Culturelpool

Culture Liverpool

MEMORIES
AUGUST
1914
23-27 JULY 2014
facebook.com/GiantSpectacular
@GiantSpectacle
giantspectacular.com
THE·MEN·OF·LIVERPOOL·WHO·FELL·IN·THE·GREAT·WAR

Liverpool City Council, 14-18 NOW and Royal de Luxe would like to extend a big thank you to all our funders and sponsors without whom this show would not have taken place.